Secrets to Life Addition and Revelation to the Bible

Perfection and Imperfection
Good and Evil

Mark F Karns

DEDICATED TO ALL PEOPLE OF GOOD WILL

This book is written to attract people of good will who give credence to what I say and want to join in and even invest in me. With enough resources my family and friends can travel to Jerusalem to bring peace and merciful justice through the hand of the Lord to the entire world.

"THE TRUTH WILL SET YOU FREE"

--John 3:32

CONTENTS

PREFACE

I was compelled to write this book to spread the true understanding of our creator God Jehovah and His son Jesus. This is necessary for all of us to use in our development. It teaches us the faith necessary to learn how to live in harmony with people of good will to bring peace to the planet. The main reason I wrote this book was because I wanted everyone to find happiness, true success, peace and security.

ACKNOWLEDGMENTS

I would like to thank the Lord for birthing me in a free country where progressive ways of kindness can exist and flourish in the midst of repressive "Gilded Age" regressive thinking. I would like to again thank all the people I acknowledged in the acknowledgement section of my first book, "The Serpent Messiah", which was a very cathartic book for me to write.

.

INTRODUCTION

As the title suggests this book is an addition and revelation to the Bible. It stresses the necessary steps needed to develop a healthy Godly psychology. By reading and understanding this book the sovereign Lord will bring other people of like psychology into your group of friends. This will give you a life of "Heaven on Earth". This book is short and to the point. Therefor the reader will quickly gain a true understanding of the way which leads to character, peace and prosperity in all things.

1 LIFE CHOICES

There are two choice we can make in our lives. We can make a decision for a blessed common sense life by acknowledging God as our source. We can also make the other choice for a self-led life without God as our source which always leads to a dead end anything goes life.

Therefor we all choose with our free will what we desire for our lives. We can choose to learn more about God and follow Him. He then will associate us with people who worship and live by His laws. We can also choose to not worship God and instead study the ways of people who choose to rebel against him. These people choose to blame Him for all of their ungodly ways by transferring their own ways to be His characteristics. The Lord will bring such people into our lives as a reminder of the problems that come with not living a righteous life.

If we choose to live in the righteous ways of God He will make us wise, caring, honest, genuine, a good example, an asset, a positive in the community, a warrior for peace, or a teacher of non-violence for peace, and He will make us intelligent and knowledgeable with insight.

If we choose to rebel against God we will acquire the ways that lead to a dead end and destruction. We will become careless, a liar, disingenuous, a hell raiser, a constant problem, a burden, a freeloader, a liability, a flaunter of wealth, an advocate of non-violence against injustice, and a negative in the community.

The choices we make in our youth (and for some people in their previous life as a spirit) affect the blessings we wish or pray for as we grow up here on Earth. For instance, my choices and words that I spoke to Eve in the Garden of Eden when I was known as the Serpent affected my character as Jesus. These same words have affected me even more as I have grown up in my life on Earth. The Lord has humbled me by these words, but he has met my every need. I consider the curse of the Lord on me from my youth as the Serpent to be the greatest blessing of all. The Lord has given me all the good characteristics of a righteous person in the last days of my life.

2 PERFECTION

It should be understood that our infinite creator Lord is the only perfect living being. The perfection of God is absolute. Everything He thinks, says and does is perfect. Since God is the infinite spirit, His spirit is in all things and He is able to read every creatures thoughts. God is all powerful, but He gives us free will which often makes us question His power and complete knowledge. We limit our understanding of the power of God the Father because He is invisible and often works in quiet subtle ways. Many people go as far as to say that God does not exist, because they cannot feel, see, or touch Him.

For the Lord's creations to be perfect they must follow all the commandments, laws, rules and regulations that our perfect creator gave Moses at Mount Saini.

We were all created perfect, but soon after our creation we became imperfect the instant we first broke one of the rules of the Lord.

The perfection of the sacrifice of Jesus as opposed to the absolute perfection of his Father rests on the foundation of the repentance of Jesus to turn his will over to the perfect Will of his Father, Jehovah. Therefor an accurate description of the many identities of Jesus, the messiah, will be given in Chapter 2 titled Imperfection. The reason a sacrifice is the needed is to atone for the un-forgivable sin. The sacrifice will redeem all repentant righteous souls to life everlasting. The destiny of oblivion and death for whoever commits the unforgivable sin allows the Lord to mercifully judge the world and sentence all evil creatures to oblivion and death. The reason that Jesus is the perfect sacrifice for the salvation of life is because he was responsible, yet not to blame, for evil. This is perfect justice. The perfect justice for the sacrifice of Jesus allows for the redemption of all souls that his Father judges righteous and worthy of life everlasting.

To suggest that Jesus is a sacrifice yet will be the eternal king and God forever is contrary to what the definition of sacrifice is. This widely held false belief has given rise to false religions and a misunderstanding of who and what God is. The Lord's wish is for all His creations to be eternally good in character and behavior.

3 IMPERFECTION

All people, including Jesus, are imperfect as finite souls. Soon after we are able to understand what we hear, the Lord consoles us on how to remain perfect by telling us the necessary decisions we need to make in order to remain perfect. It is very soon after our creation that we make a wrong decision that results in shattering any hope of remaining perfect. At the beginning of our creation we all are without experience on which to rely on when making decisions using our free will.

The first imperfect action or wrong thought after our initial creation is most commonly a doubtful unloving thought while the Lord is consoling us on the importance that we must love Him and worship only Him in order to live a long, happy, and fulfilling life. God, the Father, is merciful and forgiving. Therefor we need not continually suffer in shame for wrong thoughts. Happiness, true success, knowledge, security and love can only be experienced by continually praying with the realization that the Lord our creator is sovereign and hears our every thought.

Did Jesus remain perfect, unlike all of the other of the Lord's creations, throughout his period of growth from infancy onward throughout his life? No!

The first of the many identities of the messiah is

God's son, Mark. He was created from the spirit heart of God the Father. God's son, Mark, was given the responsibility for preparing some of the characteristics of the bodies and character of God's creations. However, most of the characteristics of God's creations came from the mind of the creator Lord, Jehovah. Mark was slow of thought and growth, but he persisted in his assigned duties.

The second identity of God's son was when Adam named him Serpent in the Garden of Eden. The Lord had placed His son Mark in the Garden of Eden to testify to Adam and Eve. The Serpent was infatuated by Eve's voice and rebelled against the advice of his Father and lied to Eve.

The Serpent, God's young child Mark, did not hate God, but suffered anxiety and shame for lying to Eve.

The third identity of the messiah was called Jesus as was described in the Bible. Jesus unwittingly told of his other identity as the false prophet in Revelations which he conveyed to John.

Hell, the Deity of Jesus, and other things were the things that qualified Jesus as the false prophet.

Many of the predictions of the ministry of Jesus have come true and will come true however.

By examining the lessons taught by the life of Jesus we can see how Jesus evolved. By reading the initial lessons

Jesus taught, and then comparing the later lessons that he taught we can see the development of Jesus. This will enable us all to see how he continued to grow and even sometimes regress during his life as his life progressed through time.

Before we are born and after we first sin, the Lord speaks to us in His most appropriate tone. He tells us of what we need to think and what we need to change in our lives in order to come back to Him with proper worship and appreciation of Him for being our most merciful creator. We should always praise God for continually restoring our souls to a more perfect state in order to be a part of His wonderful world.

4 GOOD AND EVIL

As we go from our initial ignorant state of perfection to our advancing state of imperfection with more knowledge in us, we next have to choose between good and evil. To be good we must obey the Lord when He tells us that we must seek Him in all we do.

If we try to be good by relying only on our own reasoning then we will soon learn that we can only be good and make the right decisions if we open our minds and heart to the Lord's ever-present spirit and if we faithfully study from His word and learn from the experiences He has given us.

If we do not ask the Lord to guide our minds then wrong thoughts which have come from our past wrong experiences and teachings will lead us into having a wrong character which will eventually lead to us becoming evil.

Also if we do not seek the Lord all the days of our lives then we will speak things that attract the wrong people to us, and our lives will eventually become disrupted and subject to control of ignorant or evil people.

Since none of us is God we do not know the genesis of the psyche of anyone else. I am not certain of the extent of my psyche when I was first created. My first awareness was the sound of silence and the surrounding darkness. The Lord

Jehovah spoke softly to me in a quiet reassuring voice in order to calm my fears. I gradually learned the meaning of the words that the Lord spoke to me by Him speaking the name of the body part that I was thinking of.

I respected and grew to love the voice of the Lord and appreciated the feel of His kind gentle hand as He took me to places outside of my heavenly bedroom. I remember the Lord taking me into a small play room and teaching me to play with a ball and a few other toys. The Lord used this play room for my development and it was an excellent way for Him to teach me self-control. I was obedient to the directions of the Lord, but I did start to become out of control with excitement when I was playing with the ball. That is why I believe I was created without any knowledge of evil because I thought of no evil nor did I do evil. I have however over my lifetime learned what evil is.

I may be wrong, but I believe every other living creature has a knowledge of evil as part of its mind at creation.

When I became intrigued with the loving kind young girl, Eve, I broke my promise to the Lord and lied to her.

I rationalized why I had lied to Eve, but I still did not realize that I had done evil. The Lord placed a chill in my soul for disobeying Him and for not knowing how to react to His reproof of me. I immediately felt like an outcast from God.

I knew that the Lord had reassuringly told me that I would save the world so I did not take it seriously enough when the

Lord warned me of the terrible consequences to the world if I lied to Eve.

I have changed my fear and my fight to stay alive after I said as the person known as Jesus, "It is finished.", when I was on the cross at Calvary. My mind has changed into a healthy acceptance of my death at any moment in the remaining time of what is left of my life. This will occur during my fourth and final identity as the "Son of man". This is a comfort to my soul and I no longer dwell on my terrible final destiny of death and oblivion. I no longer consider my death as unbearable like I did when I was on the cross at Calvary, but I now consider it to be perfect justice from the Lord to bring about His wonderful world to come and therefor it is quite bearable for me, now.

I believe that because all other people have a knowledge of evil, they are much more skeptical and defensive than I am. That is why they can be tempted to go to war if they feel in any way threatened.

Also, this knowledge of good and evil can be very useful as a tool for raising children because parents know what their children are thinking from remembering their own lives. This gives me great pause in wanting to raise children because I am not personally familiar with evil rebellious behavior of children.

The wonderful consequences from our sovereign creator Lord for our good thoughts and behavior have prevented madness and evil from overtaking the world.

The wrath of the Lord against un-repentant evil doers is His way of separating evil from good. Upon realizing that the Lord is sovereign and that the Lord shields His chosen people from evil doers, the evil doers lose all control and do or say anything, no matter how outrageous, to unsettle all the world and spread irrational violent behavior throughout their community of rebels against the Lord.

5 WRONG CONVENTIONAL BELIEFS ABOUT JEHOVAH AND JESUS

To proclaim belief in God among people of similar beliefs can be material rewarding in America. Actually many of these "believers" have no real understanding or faith in God and His son the messiah, Jesus.

Many people reject the true description of God and His son, Jesus, which I have presented in this book.

The elevation of the messiah to an equal position of power and character to that of God, his Father, has been devastating to America.

Even the Jehovah's Witnesses faith is wrong. Recently my Godly Jehovah witness friend attempted to correct my concept of God and His son Jesus. He is very kind and accepting of all of me except my explanation of who God is and who Jesus is. My statement to him and also what I said in church today was that God, the Lord, is the only infinite spirit who can read minds and who is sovereign in all the affairs of man.

I also stated that Jesus cannot read minds, but that the Lord can and did tell Jesus what other people were thinking. This produced the false belief among the followers of Jesus, that Jesus could read minds also.

I tried to explain to my Jehovah witness friend that Jesus was God's excellent example of how all of us should live. I did say that Jesus made mistakes in his predictions and theology. For example, Jesus said that the Lord would torment in Hell (through fire pain) the devil and all evil creatures. This is not only not true, but would make the Lord God Jehovah evil. My friend said that "torment" means to "put away" to which I said that is what Jesus will ultimately mean, but that his explanation in Revelations was unclear.

Even the Jehovah's Witnesses faith limit Jehovah's power to that of a finite spirit person. My Jehovah witness friend explained that Jehovah was an individual spirit person. He said that Jesus had been given his Father's ability to read minds and that Jesus was given authority to judge the world. Jesus is a finite being and therefor is unable to discriminately and individually judge the world. Therefor Jesus is unable to execute what a person's final eternal destination will be.

I explained that the Lord Jehovah is not a spirit person, but is the infinite sovereign spirit which indwells the world and universe in order to maintain life and order through reading our minds using His infinite power. The Lord our creator is the only being who can make a perfect merciful judgment of all creatures and who can save the world by sending to oblivion all creatures who rebel against Him and do evil.

Soon the faith of the world will be of one understanding. The people of the world will understand that they are in communication with God at all times. People will no longer be required to go through an intermediary but will still be subject to the rule of God's king, Christ. Christ is also subject to the same rules as all of the rest of the world.

Satan's power is so strong in our world that even my Jehovah witness friend would not accept my belief. I also said that even though the Bible was the inspired word of God through His son Jesus there are still mistakes in it. Although most of what Jesus predicted came true, he might be considered the false prophet which he spoke of in the Bible. He unwittingly spoke of himself. This is because of the mistakes of Jesus in his prediction of the future and the proper theology of him and his Father, the Lord Jehovah. Jesus is a humble man and will live up to his mistakes to turn his will over to the Will of his Father for him to become the perfect sacrifice for the salvation of the world.

6 THE DEGENERATION OF MERCIFUL JUSTICE AND RIGHTEOUSNESS IN AMERICA

America's freedom allows for the existing together of politicians of mostly evil (Republicans, tea party, and their supporters) and politicians of mostly good (progressive Democrats, gun law supporters, supporter of socially benevolent policies, and righteous humble lovers of God and their true righteous fellow citizens).

Washington DC recently experienced the wrath of the Lord from a rejected US Navy enlisted reserve person who may not have fallen in line with the mantra of the US Navy about the greatness of America, or especially the more radical form of jingoism that exists in America. This US Navy Veteran was mentally ill because he may have seen the evil and hypocrisy growing among the righteous claims of people in the military being led by corrupt people.

By re-watching the movies of the 1940's such as the Roy Rodger's movies, I realize my limited understanding of what the movies were telling us when I first watched them in the 1950's as a young boy. I judged the firm tone of Roy Rodgers as something to be desired to improve my passive non-assertive character. Roy Rodger's behavior was to accept people even after they made wrong decisions and let them suffer the consequences of their decisions with faith that the blame would eventually fall where it belonged.

I wrongly judged this behavior of Roy Rodger as an un-Godly uncaring attitude instead of his solid belief that the Lord would eventually bring the right judgment. For the most part, the movies of the 1940's portrayed the justice of the hand of the Lord at work in America.

I believe the movies of today do not show the hand of the Lord bringing justice and His righteousness to America as much as it did back then.

The movies of today have disrespectful talk along with idol worship and they give respect to people of bad character and violent behavior. I think this is producing a generation of Americans with no faith that justice and righteousness will prevail.

Today I see the power of the Lord in producing a righteous character in Roy Rodger. I also see Roy Rodger's trust along with the faithful trust of most of his fellow Americans in the American justice system as the basis for the Lord's blessing of America. That is why Americans must be vigilant to prevent corruption of the American justice system.

My calling from the Lord is not the same as that of the calling of Roy Rodger from the Lord. My calling is to improve the American justice system and improve the American government so that it will strengthen the hand of the Lord through better more righteous policies of justice and peace. The only way I can do this is by seeking the Lord's help at all times. I must ask Him for the strength to accept anything He brings to me including rejection and death.

For me to fulfill the Lord's assignment He gave to me before my death, I must realize that the Lord intended for me to be political minded. I cannot patronize people by pretending to agree to their policies and rhetoric that I consider evil. The Lord revealed to the world the immature nature of Jesus when Jesus rode into Jerusalem on a donkey. Jesus was unaware of the power he yielded as the Son of God at that time in his life in Jerusalem. The Lord had different plans for Jesus' life than Jesus fully realized.

Today, immediately to the north of where I live in Weld County, some irresponsible politicians are proposing for the north east corner of Colorado to succeed from Colorado and form a radical tea party state of their own. What disastrous evil that would bring.

The Lord knows that I would much prefer to retire in a world of peace to a cabin in the mountains with my family and friends to bask in their beautiful company with every peaceful thing that the Lord has provided.

However, until the raucous unrighteous Republican corporate leaders are shut down there is no place in America where anyone can experience peace and Godly living and still be safe from disruptive people that make up the corporate leadership of America.

Therefor I must remain in tune with what is going on in America and do all I can to prevent evil from crushing the freedom of people of goodness in America.

I know this sounds arrogant coming from such an

un-remarkable person like me. For this reason I am doomed to fail in the community of unbelief in America. However, as long as I hold fast to the Lord and live in His ways, I know He can use me to bring peace and goodness to America, Jerusalem and the world.

7 CHRISTIAN TELEVISION

John Hagee is a preacher on the Daystar Television Network. He assumes the role of a prophet. He attempts to predict the future. He reviles our wonderful and truly Christian president of peace. He unequivocally supports Israel regardless of whether Israel's policies are right and compassionate.

He rightly says that God will establish His headquarters for world government using Christ as King over authorities coming from the twelve tribes of Israel. Some of these chosen people for authority also have partial Palestinian heritage.

The Lord has blessed Pastor Hagee with material things because Pastor Hagee has given material things to Israel. Pastor Hagee's character is very dominating with a tone similar to that of Adolf Hitler. Therefor Pastor Hagee has not been blessed with the same insight and character as Jesus.

Marcus Lamb, the founder of Daystar Television Ministries, is giving everyone a chance to buy a small piece of land in Israel. I am putting my faith in the Lord to receive from Him a small caretaker's home next to the Temple in Jerusalem. I cannot afford to purchase the small piece of land in Israel from the Daystar Television Network. I wanted to place a small cross and Star of David with the name Serpent Messiah Jesus on them.

I have been sowing seeds of money to benevolent political and religious institutions. Therefor I am asking the Lord to bless my family and friends with His character. Then they will abundantly receive enough money necessary to fulfill their assignment from Him. I have been learning the Jewish culture and Hebrew language as my way of supporting Israel.

8 CURSES AND BLESSINGS

I thank the Lord for His ever presence to curse and bless us for any evil or good things that we do in our life. I wrote my very aware and knowledgeable Rabbi Rose about this. The following are my amended excerpts from what I wrote.

Your sermon provoked me to thought about the Lord's curse on me for my childhood sins. The curse turned out to be the greatest blessing in my life to give me peace in the waning years of my life.

The worry and anxiety resulting from my childhood sins proved to be most beneficial to me in making right decisions in my adult life. As strong as the military indoctrination of me was, I soon felt the anxiety from my sins and militant malevolent behavior that it brought on in me.

As strongly as the idea of never having to say you are sorry was brought out in boot camp, my desire to be healed through repentance was placed deep within my soul by the Lord and from other sailor's testimony.

Thus the curse of the Lord for my childhood sins was a great deterrent against me doing wrong during my young adult years. The Lord's faithfulness to me by calling me through a rock when I was a boy of four years old was probably the greatest force that kept my faith as I lived my life.

The beginning of the Lords curse on me began with my lie to Eve in the Garden of Eden. The anxiety deep within my soul from my rebellion against the Lord and against Eve in the Garden of Eden has left me now. Therefor thankfully it can be replaced with the blessing of a peaceful feeling of acceptance of the Lord's judgment of death for me at any time.

I no longer dwell on my final destiny of oblivion, but focus on the things I can do every day to advance peace in the world and put praise for the Lord on the lips of as many people as I can.

I thank the Lord for people like Mark in the parts department at Sillterhar Volvo. He saves me money on parts by recommending only parts that I need. By doing this he produces a responsible business for the benefit of the community.

Sillterhar Volvo caters to the needs of its customers and employees by providing comfortable waiting areas with free water and pop and pleasant people to do business and visit with. Doing business at Sillterhar Volvo with people like Mark has been a blessing.

The blessing of the Lord by His prevention of the spread of knowledge about me being the Serpent Messiah Jesus has protected me from violent mortal danger all my life. I have strictly managed the necessary things I have needed to do to remain humble and within the will of the Lord.

I praise the Lord for those things, and I am most willing to accept what He has in store for me now. I know that the day of my eternal death is very close, but I give thanks to the Lord that He has not told me when my death will occur so that I can wake up each day with anticipation of what the Lord will bring to me. I can give Him my appreciation for the days of my life that I have left.

9 THE LORD JEHOVAH: MASTER OF WEATHER NOT "MOTHER NATURE"

When I tell people the Lord is the sovereign master of weather which includes floods, tornadoes, blizzards, thunder and lightning, they often reject that. It could be because I am an unremarkable common citizen, or it could be out of apathy and wanting to remain ignorant. Also it could be because people do not want to accept the tragic deaths resulting from these extreme weather conditions as coming from the hand of the Lord.

Death comes at the perfect stage in any life for its own good and the good of the world.

SUMMARY

THE SECRETS TO LIFE IN A NUTSHELL

The secret to life in a nutshell is to know what God is and His character. To know God and truth we must continually seek him all the days of our lives, and ask Him to put words in our mouths to praise Him and spread good will among the people we speak to. We must never think, speak or do evil. We must continually read the Bible to learn how to live our lives by leaning the rules that God has laid out for us and to learn more about the people God chose in the world.

ABOUT THE AUTHOR

The authors Earthly life began in 1944 by being incarnated from a spirit being into his mother's womb. He was called in the flesh by the Lord God Almighty of Israel, sovereign of the Universe, through a rock in the foothills overlooking Denver, Colorado at the age of 4 years. He learned of the awesomeness of the Creator's world as an assistant marine biologist tagging salmon in the Gulf of Alaska and the Bering Sea during the early 1960's. He spent most of his life after being discharged from the US Navy allowing himself to be submitted to brain retarding drugs. Even though brain damaged as a child from medical operations, the Lord God Almighty partially restored him so that he could remember and recount the events of his childhood and life in this book and his other book "The Serpent Messiah".

www.ingramcontent.com/pod-product-compliance
Lightning Source LLC
Chambersburg PA
CBHW070934290526
45795CB00003B/1018